CONTENTS

GW01465781

CAMBRIDGE UNIVERSITY PRESS
Cambridge
New York   New Rochelle
Melbourne   Sydney

INTRODUCTION

The purpose of this book is to give all those reading it a greater understanding of the laws of Rugby Football. The laws themselves are essential to the game, and once understood, they allow players to improve their play and so enjoy the game even more.

The game of Rugby Football is supposed to have originated through the actions of a schoolboy called William Webb Ellis. In 1823, while playing a game of football at Rugby School, he broke the rules by picking up the ball and running with it.

Whether or not this is true is a matter for argument. However by 1880 the governing bodies of Rugby had been formed in England (1871) Scotland (1873) Ireland (1874) and Wales (1880). Around the turn of the century a split developed between a number of northern clubs and the rest of the Rugby-playing clubs in England, which resulted in the formation of the professional game of Rugby League. However, the strictly amateur game of Rugby Union continued to be developed, and by 1910 an International Championship was under way. Since then each of the British nations, as well as France in more recent years, have enjoyed periods of dominance over their rivals.

The first ever international match was played between Scotland and England in 1871 and these two countries have remained arch rivals ever since. Each season they play for the Calcutta Cup.

This cup was presented to the Rugby Football Union in 1878 by the members of the Calcutta Rugby Club. Owing to the lack of support the members decided to disband the club and have the silver rupees in their bank account melted down to form this famous trophy.

By the 1870s Rugby was being played in Australia, South Africa and New Zealand. In New Zealand, Rugby was soon to become the national sport and during the period 1900 to 1930 they were the premier Rugby-playing nation of the world. In particular the 1924 team which toured Britain earned the title 'The Invincibles' after winning every match they played. Since that period of superiority the 'All Blacks', as they are called, have maintained their international dominance. It is easy to understand why they are such feared opponents when you see them perform a 'haka', a kind of war-dance, before a match. This Maori war-dance was originally intended to put fear into the hearts of the enemy.

The British Lions playing against New Zealand – a ruck forming.

The only country to have matched the Rugby power of New Zealand over the years is South Africa (the Springboks). Their international sides have been difficult opponents on tour and almost unbeatable on their own ground. During the period 1921–1956 even the best of the All Black sides were unable to beat them. Even the 'British Lions', which is the touring side combining the best players from England, Ireland, Scotland and Wales, have found them to be extremely difficult opponents.

Although Australia has never enjoyed the same dominance as South African or New Zealand counterparts, they are amongst the premier Rugby-playing nations of the World. As early as 1875 the forerunner of the Australian RFU was formed and since then the fast-moving running and passing game, characteristic of Australian Rugby, has continued to develop. Perhaps the chief reason why Australian Rugby has not dominated international competition is that Rugby has remained a relatively minor sport within the country.

Apart from the countries mentioned Rugby is played extensively in Canada, USA, Fiji, Japan, Argentina, Italy, Romania and to a lesser extent in more than fifty other countries throughout the world – a truly international sport.

WHAT IS RUGBY?

Rugby is a fast, exciting and enjoyable game which requires a great deal of effort from all the players involved. It is important therefore if you are to play well that you make every effort to:
- understand the laws and how they affect the game
- train hard and so become physically fit
- learn and practise the skills involved

Once you have combined the above points you will be able to play to the best of your ability, and so gain a great deal of enjoyment from one of the most exciting ball games in the world.

The teams

Each team is made up of 8 forwards and 7 backs. The forwards, often called *the pack* (because they hunt as a pack so as to win the ball), act as a unit at all times. Their job is to:
- win the ball and give it to the backs (their most important job)
- support the man on their team who has hold of the ball
- take part in *scrummages, line-outs, rucks* and *mauls*

The drawing shows a set of forwards, in their positions, waiting to take part in a scrummage. Their numbers are given.

Back row

Second row

Front row

Forwards in action in mini-rugby.

The backs

The backs are made up of

No. 9 – Scrum half	These players shape the pattern of play, deciding how and where to attack the opposition's defensive line
No. 10 – Outside half (or fly half)	
No. 11 – Left wing	These players act as the main attacking and defensive unit
No. 12 – Centre	
No. 13 – Centre	
No. 14 – Right wing	
No. 15 – Full back	This player acts as an extra attacking player and also a covering defensive player

The main job of the backs is to break through the opponents' defence and score *tries*. However they also have to stop the opposition who are trying to do exactly the same.

The laws do not say where players should stand but there are certain regular arrangements. The backs always line up behind their forwards so that if the forwards win the ball it can be passed back to them to provide an opportunity for breaking through the opposition's defence. The position of the forwards on the pitch at any time will determine how the backs line up; however, in general the backs will adopt an attacking pattern if their forwards are likely to win a ball or a defensive pattern if they are not.

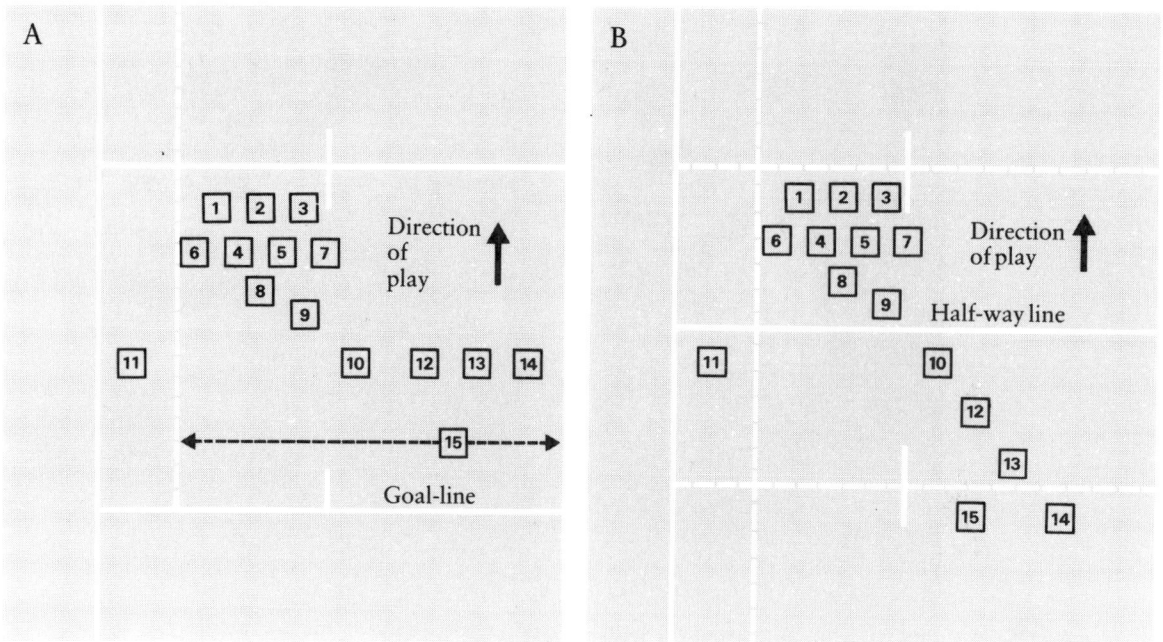

(A) This is the defensive set-up (notice that the full back, no. 15, acts as a covering player for his defensive line).

(B) This is the attacking set-up (notice how the players are positioned so as to run on to the ball when it is passed back towards them; also note that no. 15 is poised to come into the line and act as an extra attacker at a moment's notice).

Scoring a try

Scoring is simple. Within the 40 minutes allowed for each half of the game, each team attempts to *ground* the ball (press it into the ground from above) beyond their opponent's *goal-line*. It is important to remember that the ball must be pressed into the ground from above.

Grounding the ball on or beyond your opponents' goal-line is worth 4 points.

Remember, if you cross the goal-line, always try to ground the ball behind the posts, as in (a) in the drawing. This makes the conversion easier for your kicker.

Once you have scored a try you are allowed a kick at goal (a *conversion*) and this is worth 2 points. The kick, a *place* or *drop kick*, is taken anywhere along a line through the point where the try was scored.

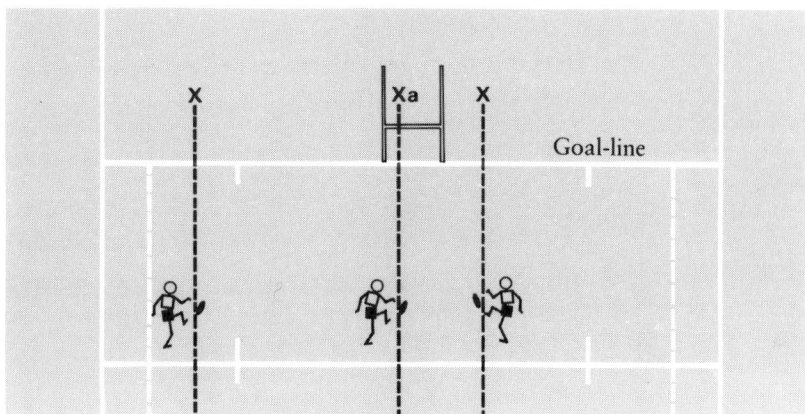

The tries were scored at the points indicated with an X and so in each case the conversion can be taken anywhere along the line shown.

Scoring from a drop goal

In addition to scoring a try, you may score from a *drop goal*. This is worth 3 points and happens during play when the ball is dropped from the hands and kicked over the crossbar on the half volley.

Scoring from a penalty

Finally you may be awarded a penalty. From this you can kick directly for goal as in the conversion. A penalty goal is worth 3 points.

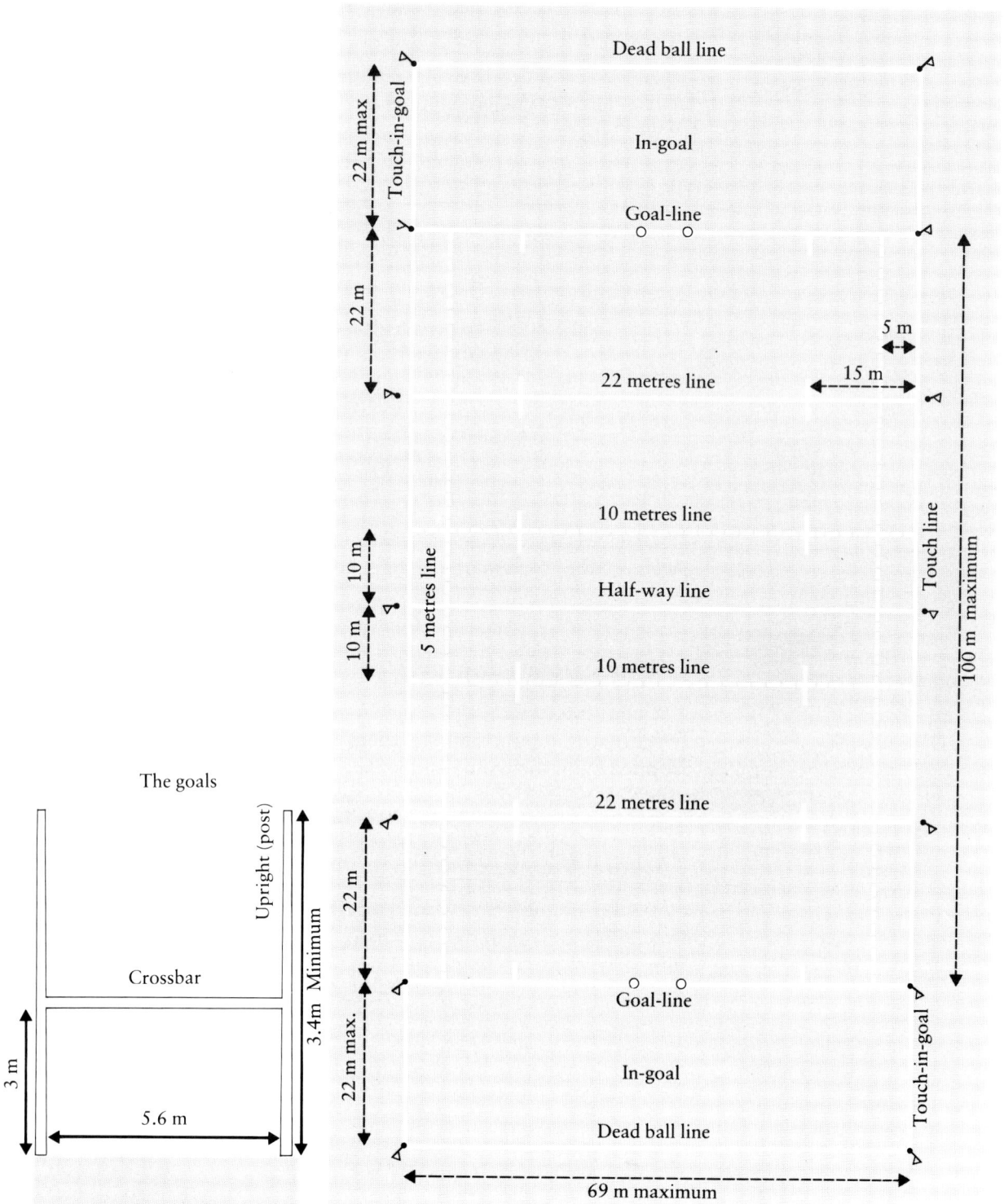

THE PITCH

Dead ball line

Touch-in-goal

22 m max

In-goal

Goal-line

22 m

22 metres line

5 m

15 m

10 metres line

5 metres line

10 m

10 m

Half-way line

10 metres line

Touch line

100 m maximum

22 metres line

22 m

Goal-line

22 m max.

In-goal

Touch-in-goal

Dead ball line

69 m maximum

The goals

Upright (post)

Crossbar

3.4m Minimum

3 m

5.6 m

Remember, 'the field-of-play' is bordered by, but does not include, the *touch lines* or the goal-lines. If you put your foot on the touch line when you are carrying the ball, it is out of play. If you put the ball down on your opponents' goal-line it is a try.

What the markings mean

- *Dead ball line* – this means what it says. When the ball touches or passes over this line it becomes dead. Therefore we cannot score a try if we ground the ball on this line.
- *Touch lines and touch-in-goal lines* – when the ball touches or passes over these lines it is out of play. Therefore we cannot score a try if we ground the ball on a touch-in-goal line.
- *Goal-line* – to score a try we need to ground the ball on this line or anywhere in the in-goal area other than on the dead ball line or the touch-in-goal line.
- *22 metres line* – this line is the limit of a defensive sanctuary. In this area defenders are given certain privileges while playing.
- *10 metres line* – this line is used by the players at the *kick-off*.
- *Half-way line* – this line is used as the starting-point for the game and for all restarts after points have been scored.
- *5 metres line* (parallel with the touch line) – this is used by the forwards at *line-outs*.
- *15 metres marks* (parallel with the touch lines) – these are also used by the forwards at line-outs.
- *In-goal* – this area where we score tries is of vital importance.
- *The goal* – this acts as the target for all kicking attempts when trying to score points.

Cardiff Arms Park, Wales.

ADVANTAGE — THE MOST IMPORTANT LAW

Now that we understand the positions, the players, the markings and how to score, we are ready to learn to play the game correctly according to the laws. If you break any of the laws the referee will blow his whistle to stop the game unless advantage is being played.

Unlike some other games breaking the law during a game of Rugby does not necessarily mean the referee will blow his whistle and stop the game. Instead, the referee waits to see whether or not the team who were not at fault can gain an *advantage* from the situation that results. If they do appear to gain an advantage, he lets the game go on; if they do not, he blows his whistle to stop the game and he makes his decision as if the original offence had just taken place. You must therefore remember when playing Rugby to *play to the whistle*. This means that even though you may see an offence taking place you do not stop and wait for the whistle. Neither do you appeal. You just get on with the game until you do hear the whistle.

There are two types of advantage.

Play on until you hear the whistle.

Territorial advantage

This occurs when you gain ground or get the ball closer to your opponents' goal-line. In the drawing, the dark-shirted team are attacking, but a bad pass from A makes B *knock on* and drop the ball. The ball is kicked ahead and followed up by E on the other side. The referee does not stop the game for the knock-on (an offence, as we will see later) but allows the game to go on because the other side have gained ground and therefore territorial advantage.

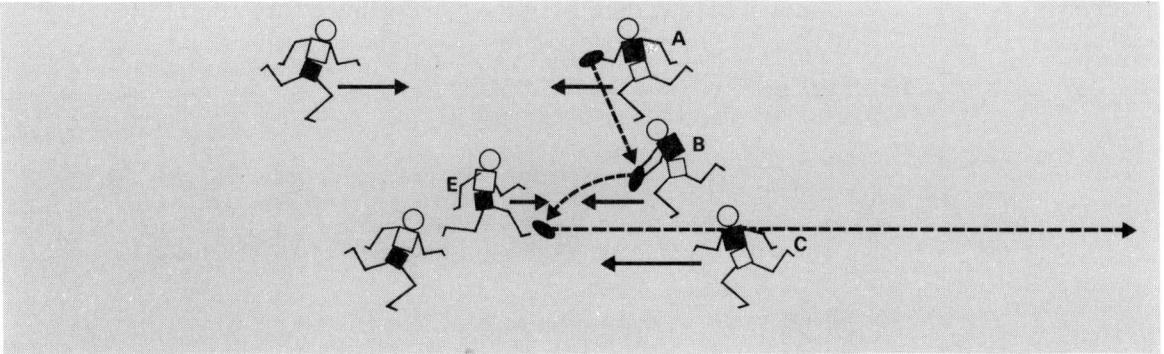

Tactical advantage

This is the opportunity to gain ground. In most situations where the referee has played advantage, the team who were not at fault will have gained ground and therefore territorial advantage. Tactical advantage means you are likely to gain territorial advantage.

Still, there are times when the advantage law cannot be used:
- When the ball comes out of either end of the tunnel at a scrummage and it has not been played.
- When either the ball or the player with the ball touches the referee.

    If the above does happen and one team does gain an advantage the referee will stop the game. The game will be restarted with a scrummage, the *put-in* being given to the team who last played the ball.

    Remember that the referee may be thought of as part of the field-of-play, so do not stop if the ball touches the referee. Keep playing until the whistle goes.
- When a player is *accidentally* offside. The referee will only stop the game if the offside player's team gain an advantage.

STARTING THE GAME

The kick-off

The game starts with a kick at the mid-point of the half-way line. If you take the kick from the wrong spot, or you use the wrong kick, the referee will tell you to take the kick again.

The direction of play, *or the chance to take the kick-off*, is decided by the captain who wins the toss. It is at the kick-off that both sets of forwards (nos. 1 to 8) usually take up the positions as shown below, the rest of the players lining up to cover the rest of

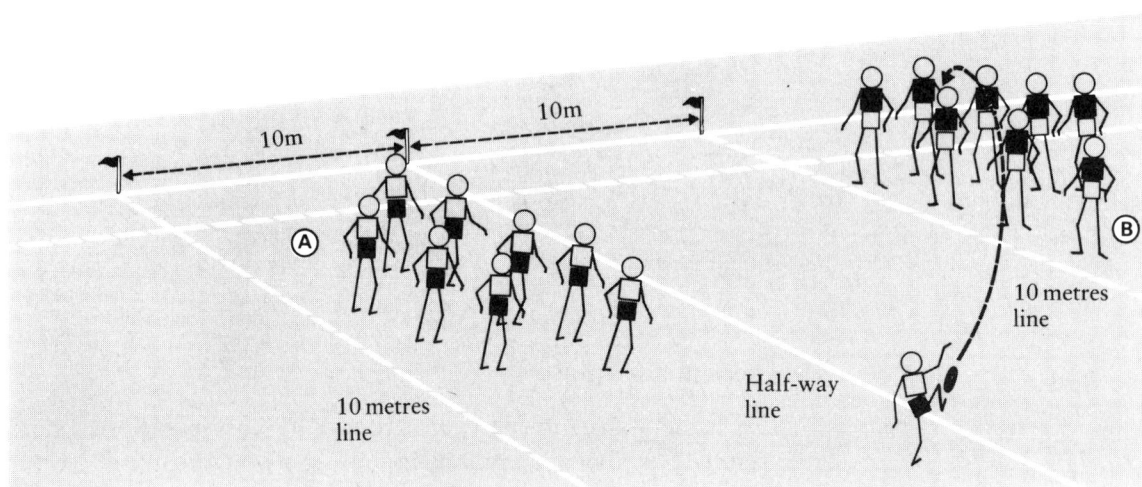

the pitch. The team A must be behind the line of the kicker when he takes the kick. If any of the team are in front of the kicker the opposition are given the put-in at a scrummage at the centre.

The opposing team B must be on or beyond the 10 metres line. If they are too near, team A take the kick again.

The kick itself is always a place kick unless the score was an unconverted try. Then it is a drop kick. The ball must go beyond the 10 metres line unless one of the other team rushes forward and touches it first, and not straight off the field unless it has bounced or touched one of the other team. If the kick does not go 10 metres the opposition choose either to have team A take the kick again, or they have the put-in at a scrummage at the centre. If the kick goes straight out of play the opposition can choose either of these, or they let the kick stand, in which case the game is restarted with a line-out at the half-way line, or at the place where the ball went out of play if this is nearer their opponents' goal-line.

It may seem silly, but the team who have the kick-off deliberately kick the ball towards their opponents, whether it be in the usual fashion where it is kicked towards the opposing forwards, or where it is kicked into a space within the opposition's half of the field. If we look at the situation we may find the kick-off not as silly as it seems. If team A take the kick, their forwards are obviously running forward while team B have to stand and wait for the ball to come to them. This means that if the kick is good enough to allow team A to get underneath the ball before it reaches their opponents they will have the added advantage of challenging for the ball while moving at speed.

Whether kicking for touch, for points or simply taking the kick-off the advice is the same – be well balanced and keep your eyes on the ball.

ATTACK AND DEFENCE

Now that the game has started, the team who win the ball attempt to move the ball towards their opponents' goal-line. They can either pass, carry or kick the ball; however, in order to keep possession it is normally safer to pass and carry the ball than to kick it towards the opposition. Players are only allowed to pass the ball backwards or sideways, as shown below.

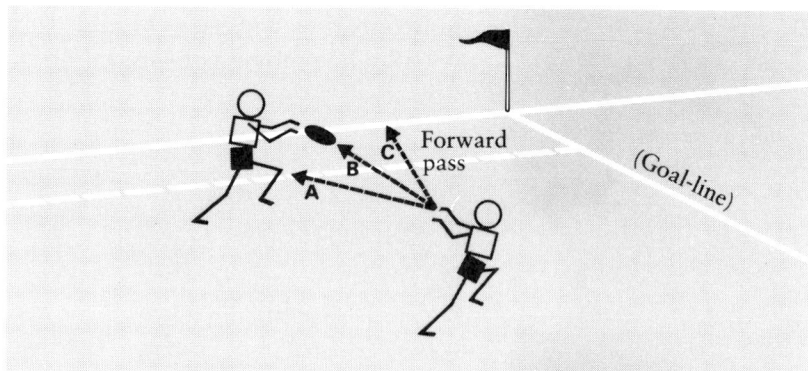

In the drawing A and B are good passes, but C is a *forward pass*. Any pass which goes towards the other team's dead ball line is a forward pass. If you make a forward pass, the opposition have the put-in at a scrummage at the point where the pass was made.

Preparing to pass.

A knock-on

This is where you mess up a pass, or where a bad pass from a team mate makes you drop the ball so that it bounces from your hand or arm towards the other team's dead ball line. (If you knock on, the opposition have the put-in at a scrummage at the point where you knocked on.)

However, there are two occasions when you can knock on yet still get away with it. These are when you are charging down an opponent's kick, or if you fumble with a catch but still gather the ball before it touches the ground or another player.

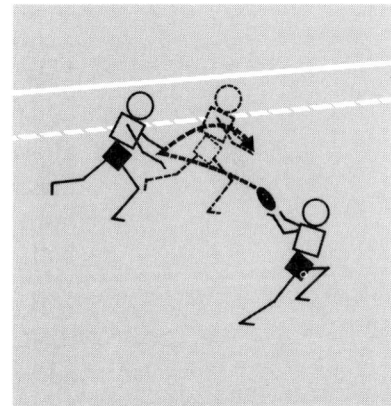

What is a tackle?

The first, and one of the most important things to remember, is that in trying to stop the opposite team from scoring you do not always *tackle*. You often push, pull or shoulder them, depending on the situation. A tackle is when you hold the man carrying the ball by any part of his body or clothing so that while you are holding him he is brought to the ground or the ball hits the ground. Bringing the man to the ground means that while holding him you will have made him fall into one of the following positions:

- onto one knee
- onto both knees
- into a sitting position
- on top of another player
- flat out along the ground

Remember: when you tackle, hold on to him and bring him to the ground.

'What has tackling to do with attacking play?', you may ask. Well, the answer is simple. The attack does not stop when you are tackled, so you need to know what to do with the ball when you are tackled either correctly or incorrectly.

When *tackled correctly* you must release the ball immediately. This also includes putting the ball on the ground, as long as it is done immediately. You should therefore try when you are tackled to twist your body towards your team mates so that when you release the ball it is on your side and not your opponents'. In addition, while lying on the ground you must not play the ball in any way. If you don't let go of the ball, or you let go and then fight for it before getting up, the opposition will be given a penalty from the spot where the incident happened. The only exception to this law is when, although tackled correctly, at the same instant you are knocked over your opponents' goal-line and a try is scored.

When *tackled incorrectly*, so that you are not held but only pushed or knocked over, you can still keep on running even if the ball has hit the ground. However, you must get up; you are not allowed to crawl around with the ball. In addition, if an opponent lifts you off your feet, this is not a tackle, because you have not been brought to the ground, so there is no need to let go of the ball.

If the person who is correctly tackled has to release the ball, then it is only fair that the tackler must allow him to do so. In addition, the tackler must not try to take the ball before it has been released, and since the person who has been tackled is not allowed to play the ball while he is on the ground then neither is the man doing the tackling; nor is the man doing the tackling allowed to stop his opponent from getting up. If the tackler does any of these things, the opposition will be given a penalty from the spot where the incident happened. Remember, if you are tackled or tackling, to leave the ball until you get back on to your feet.

DEFENDING THE GOAL-LINE

The diagram below shows one end of the pitch, which can be split up into two main areas: the 22 metres zone which is discussed in detail in relation to kicking and the in-goal area, which is the darker-shaded area in the diagram.

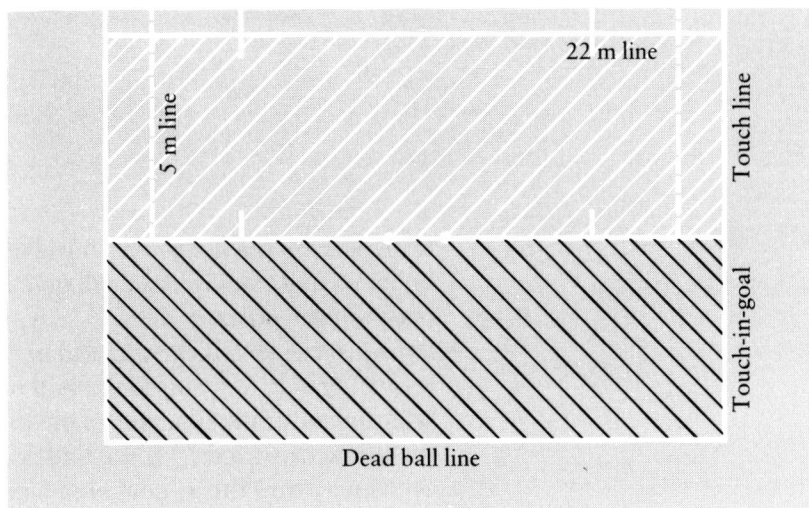

For a team on the defensive, these areas make up the danger zone and so it is vital that all players should know the results of certain actions which might be taken in these areas. However, before this, we need to know the meanings of certain words and phrases.

- *grounding the ball* – this is where a player while holding the ball, brings the ball into contact with the ground, or, while the ball is on the ground, puts a downward pressure on the ball using the front of his upper body.
- *try* – a try is scored when an on-side player grounds the ball in his opponents' in-goal by either of the methods described above.
- *touch-down* – is when a player grounds the ball in his own in-goal. The ball is then dead, as it is when it is out of play.
- *penalty try* – is awarded when foul play by the defending team stops the attacking side from scoring a probable try or from grounding the ball in a more favourable position. A penalty try is always given as if it had been scored right between the posts, therefore allowing for the simplest of conversion attempts.

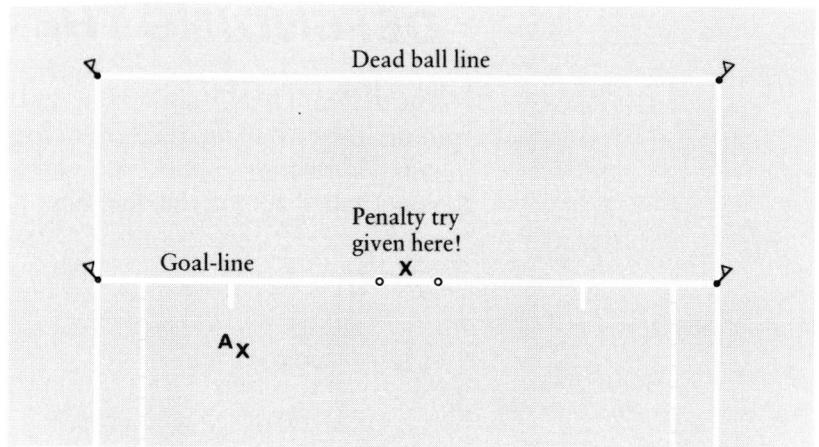

Foul play by the defence at A prevents an almost certain try being scored. The referee will give a penalty try to the other side between the posts.

- *a drop-out* – this is the method of restarting the game after the attacking side has caused the ball to go over their opponents' goal-line and someone has made the ball dead. (This does not include scoring a try.) If the ball accidentally touches a defender on its way into the in-goal area a drop-out is still awarded. As the name suggests the type of kick we use is a drop kick and in order to restart the game this kick can be taken on or behind the 22 metres line. The line acts as a barrier between the teams, with the defending side having to stay behind the ball. If any of the defending side are in front of the ball the game restarts with a scrummage at the centre of the 22 metres line, the attacking side having the put-in. The attacking side must stay their side of the line until the ball is kicked. If they step over the line before the ball is kicked, the kick is taken again. However, if the ball when kicked does not reach the 22 metres line, the opposition chooses between having the kick taken again or having the put-in at a scrummage at the centre of the 22 metres line. If the ball goes straight into *touch*, the opposition can choose either of these, or they can let the kick stand. In this case, they will then have the throw-in at a line-out.
- *a 5-metre scrummage* – a scrummage 5 metres from either goal-line. For an explanation of this, refer to the section on the scrummage later.

Whatever action we may take, then, in and around the danger zone, whether we be attackers or defenders, is of vital importance. The table setting out possible actions and what happens as a result of these actions will enable you to understand better your attacking or defensive role.

Action by a player	Restart with
● An attacking player carries or kicks the ball over the goal-line and it is	
(a) grounded by the player himself or a member of his team	(a) Try scored, conversion to follow.
(b) touched down by a defending player.	(b) 22 metres drop-out.
● A defending player carries, passes, kicks or knocks the ball over his own goal-line and it is	
(a) touched down by the player himself or a member of his team	(a) A scrummage 5 metres from the goal-line opposite the place where the ball, or a player carrying it, crossed the goal-line. Attacking side to put in.
(b) grounded by an attacking player.	(b) Try scored, conversion to follow.
● An attacking player in the in-goal area is so held that he cannot ground the ball.	A scrummage 5 metres from the goal-line opposite the place where the ball was held. Attacking side to put in.
● A defending player in the in-goal area is so held that he cannot touch the ball down.	A scrummage 5 metres from the goal-line opposite the place where the ball was held. Attacking side to put in.
● An attacking player carries, kicks or knocks the ball over the goal-line and it becomes dead e.g. when it goes over the dead ball line.	22 metres drop-out.
● A defending player carries, kicks or knocks the ball over the goal-line and it becomes dead.	A scrummage 5 metres from the goal-line. Attacking side to put in.
● A defending player carries the ball into his own in-goal area and then tries to kick the ball, but has it charged down by an attacking player, and	

Action by a player	Restart with
(a) the ball then becomes dead or is touched down or	(a) A scrummage 5 metres from the goal-line. Attacking side to put in.
(b) the ball is grounded by an attacking player.	(b) Try scored, conversion to follow.
• At a scrummage, or a ruck	
(a) The defending team with the ball in their possession are pushed over their own goal-line and a defender touches the ball down before it comes out of the scrummage or ruck	(a) A scrummage 5 metres from the goal-line. Attacking side to put in.
(b) The attacking side with the ball in their possession push back their opponents till the ball crosses over the goal-line and an attacker grounds the ball.	(b) Try scored, conversion to follow.
• Foul play by the attacking side which results in a try being scored.	Try disallowed, 22 metres drop-out. As well as disallowing the try, the referee may caution or send off the player responsible and award a penalty kick to the defending side to be taken anywhere on the 22 metres line.
• Foul play by the defending side which prevents a probable try being scored.	Penalty try awarded, conversion to follow. The referee may also caution or send off the player responsible for the foul play.
• Foul play by either side while the ball is out of play.	Penalty kick from the place where the game would have restarted. Also, the offending player may be cautioned or sent off.
• Deliberately charging (obstructing), inside in-goal, a defending player who has just kicked the ball.	A 22 metres drop-out or a penalty kick from where the ball lands. Also, the offending player may be cautioned or sent off.

Loose ball?

Mark

Another method of defending the goal-line is when a player makes a fair catch (mark). He is allowed to do this when he is inside his own 22 metres line. However, certain rules apply to making a fair catch.

- the ball must be caught cleanly from a kick, knock-on or throw forward by the other side
- the player must be standing still
- both the player's feet must be on the ground
- the player must shout 'Mark!' at the same time as he catches the ball

When a mark is awarded the game is restarted by a *free kick*. The kick is taken by the player who called for the mark, from the point where he caught the ball. When calling for a mark, the defender is often under severe pressure from the attacking side, and hence the chances of the player calling for the mark being injured are greatly increased. If that unfortunate situation occurs and the player is injured he is allowed one minute to take the kick. If this is not possible, a scrummage is formed at the point where the mark was called, with the defending side having the put-in.

Loose ball

One other aspect of play which occurs usually during the defence of the goal-line is having to fall on to a loose ball in order to secure possession for your team. However, if you are lying down holding the ball you *must*

- immediately pass the ball, or
- release the ball, or
- roll away from the ball, or
- get up onto your feet

In addition, if you are on the ground, you must not prevent any opponent gaining possession of it. If you are on your feet and you see a player lying on the ground in possession of the ball or you see the ball in the process of emerging from a ruck, you must not fall on or over the player or the ball. If you are guilty of any offence related to the loose ball the other side will be given a penalty kick from the place where you were at fault.

Remember, when the ball is on the ground, act quickly!

KICKING

The ability to kick the ball accurately and with the correct amount of force is a very important part of both good attacking and good defensive play. Kicking can also be used as a method of scoring.

The kick most often used during a game of rugby is the *punt*, where the ball is kicked out of the hands. Unlike passing, the ball can be kicked in any direction.

Once you have kicked the ball the game continues unless it is stopped for some reason, or unless the ball has gone out of play. When we kick the ball or knock it in such a way that it goes out of play at the touch lines, the game is restarted with a line-out, the throw-in being given to the opposition.

Where the line-out takes place can be decided by asking three questions:

1. Did the ball bounce first before it crossed the touch line?

    If the ball is played by any player and it bounces before it crosses the touch line, the game is restarted with a line-out at the place where the ball made contact with or crossed the touch line, the opposition having the put-in.

2. Did the ball go directly into *touch* without bouncing?

    If the ball is played by any player and it goes straight into touch, the game is restarted with a line-out at the point on the touch line opposite to where the player played the ball, the opposition having the put-in. This means that an inaccurate kick which goes straight into touch without bouncing will gain no ground whatsoever. In fact, if the point where the ball enters touch is closer to your own goal-line than the place from where you kicked it, then the line-out will take place where the ball went into touch and you will lose ground. This sometimes happens on very windy days.

3. Whoever kicked the ball, was he standing within his own 22 metres line?

    The laws of Rugby allow defending players to kick the ball directly into touch (without bouncing) only while they are within their 22 metres line. 'Within your 22 metres line' means the area bounded by the touch lines, your goal-line and your 22 metres line. If you are a defending player and you are anywhere within this area and you kick the ball directly into touch without bouncing, the game will be restarted with a line-out at the place where the ball crossed the touch line, the opposition having the put-in.

The diagram shows a player playing the ball, and in each case the ball crosses the touch line. In each case the game is restarted with a line-out, the put-in being given to the opposition. Where the line-out takes place is decided by asking the three questions.

With the kicker within his own 22 metres line the line-out is taken where the ball leaves the field of play – whether the ball bounces first or not. With the kicker outside his own 22 metres line the line-out for A and D (where the ball does not bounce before leaving the field of play) is taken in line with the kicker.

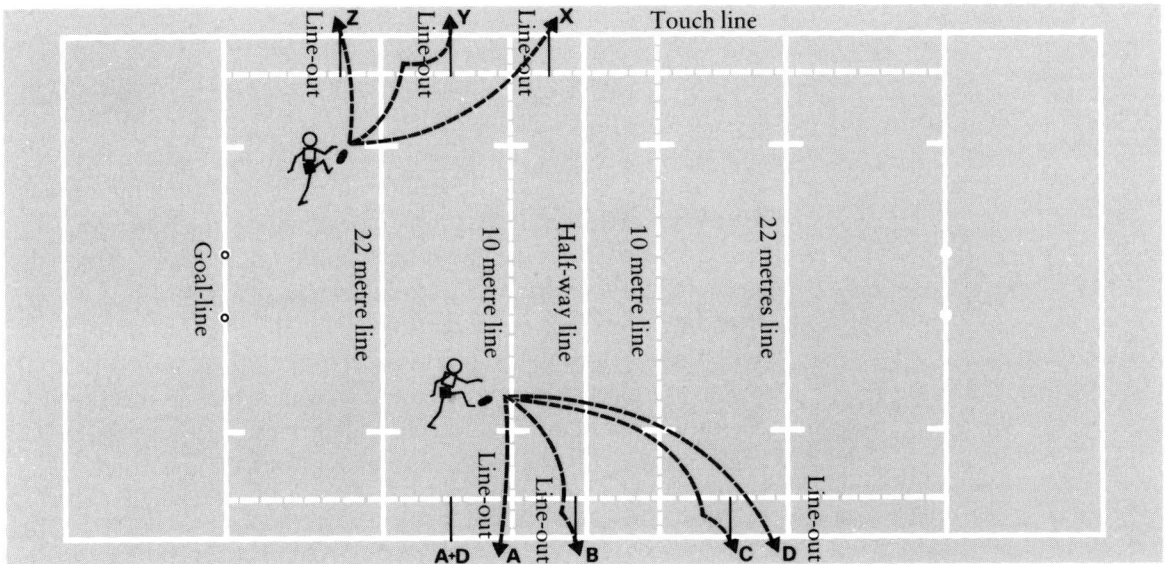

Remember, when you are outside your 22 metres line, kicking straight into touch will not gain ground. You must try to kick the ball so that it bounces first before crossing the touch line.

The place kick

Another type of kick is the place kick, where we kick the ball after we have deliberately placed it on the ground. This is when it often appears that the kicker is trying to dig up the pitch with his boot, when, in fact, he is producing a platform which will allow him to kick the ball more effectively.

Other kicks

Another type of kick is the drop kick where we let the ball fall from our hands to the ground and kick it as it bounces up. Apart from the types of kick mentioned there are other types of kick such as the *grubber*, the *chip* and the *up and under* which are invaluable in certain situations. They are all legal types of kick.

PENALTY KICKS, FREE KICKS AND CONVERSIONS

As we have already discovered, accidentally breaking the law by knocking on or passing forward gives the other side the put-in at a scrummage at the place where the law was broken. However, for more serious law-breaking (dangerous tackling, offside, tripping, etc.), the other side are given a penalty kick or the put-in at a scrummage if they want it. However it is very rare that a team will choose a scrummage in preference to a penalty kick, as a scrummage allows the other side the opportunity to win back the ball.

The referee's signal for a penalty kick is an arm held straight in the air. When a penalty kick is given the referee will point to a mark. All this means is the place on the pitch from where the penalty must be taken. At the penalty kick, if you are a member of the team who are at fault you must comply with the following.

- Run as quickly as you can to, or beyond, an imaginary line 10 metres from the mark and parallel to your own goal-line depending on which is nearest to the mark. If you don't move back quickly enough the referee will move the penalty a further 10 metres unless this means you will come within 5 metres of your own goal-line, in which case the referee will give the mark 5 metres from the goal-line. No penalty kick can be taken within 5 metres of either goal-line.

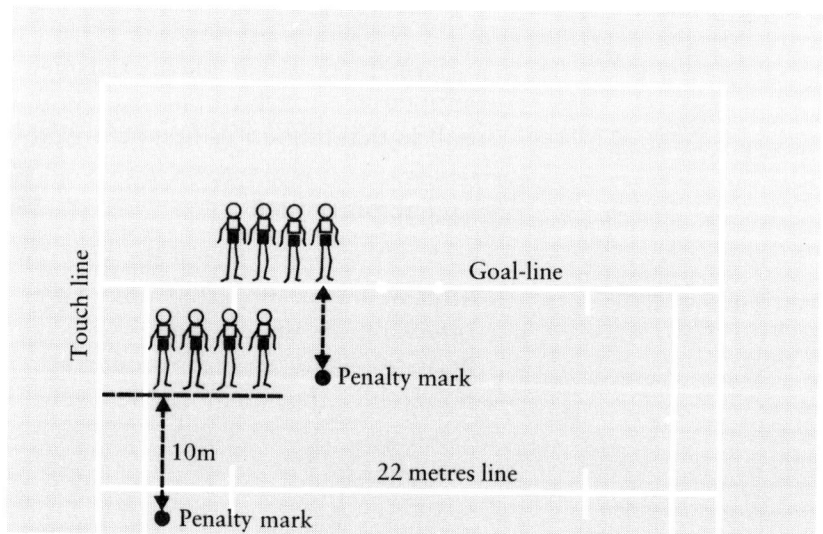

- Stand still and silent until the kick is taken. If you don't stand still or you try to put the kicker off in some way the referee will move the penalty on a further 10 metres as described before.

- If the other team take the kick quickly and you are not 10 metres from the mark the referee will not stop the game since the fact that you are within 10 metres of the mark is due to the speed at which the kick was taken and the game restarted. However, you are not allowed to take part in the game again until you have gone back 10 metres, or a member of the other team has run with the ball for 5 metres.

Remember to get back quickly and always face the ball to avoid being taken by surprise!

If, on the other hand, you are a member of the team taking the penalty then you must remember the following.
- Take the kick without wasting time. (You are allowed approximately one minute if you decide to kick at goal.)
- Take the kick at or behind the mark on a line parallel with the touch lines.
- Anybody in the team can take the kick.
- Everyone in the team must be behind the ball while the kick is being taken, except when a placer is used. A placer is a team mate who while lying on the ground steadies the ball with his finger so that a team mate can take a place kick. A placer is not normally used unless the playing conditions are poor, such as on a very windy day when the ball might blow away before it is kicked.
- Any type of kick, including a drop kick, can be used as long as when holding the ball it is kicked out of the hands, and when the ball is on the ground it is kicked at least a short distance from the mark.
- The ball can be kicked in any direction to any player.
- The kicker can also play the ball himself once he has kicked it unless he has already told the referee that he wishes to take a kick at the goal. Once this decision has been made, the kicker cannot change his mind.

If you do not kick the ball correctly, or you take too long, or someone gets in front of the ball, or you do not take the kick at the correct place, the referee will award a scrummage at the mark with the other side putting the ball in.

There are three likely kicks to use.
(a) A punt – which hopefully will go into touch so as to move play further upfield away from your defensive area. From a penalty the ball can be kicked directly into touch, no matter where the kick was taken from.
(b) When you are within kicking distance of the goals a place or drop kick, which if successful will score 3 points.

(c) When the opposition are not alert and you can take them by surprise, a *tap* is followed by gathering the ball, then running, kicking or passing (a tap is where we gently play the ball with the foot).

Kicking for touch.

Free kick

The referee's signal for this is a bent arm extended. This type of kick is awarded when the offence committed by the opposition is not serious enough to permit the award of a penalty kick, yet still avoidable and hence more serious an offence than a knock-on or a forward pass. Unlike in penalty kick situations, a goal cannot be scored by the kicker unless the ball has first been played by another player. This is why we often see the ball being tapped first by one player, who then passes the ball to a team mate, who then attempts a drop goal when within kicking distance of the goals.

Other than that, all the laws that apply to the penalty kick apply to the free kick except that the defending side having gone back 10 metres can charge the kicker as soon as he has begun to run, or made a gesture that he is about to kick the ball. If you do not take the kick at or behind the mark or the kick is not valid, meaning it has been fairly charged down and the kick prevented, the opposition are given the put-in at a scrummage at the mark. For an offence by the opposition at the free kick, such as charging too early or delaying the kick being taken, the referee will give the kicking team a penalty kick 10 metres in front of the mark. Remember, treat a free kick like a penalty. If you are a defender remember you can charge the kick. If you are an attacker remember that you cannot kick directly for goal.

Conversion

After a try has been scored you are allowed a kick at goal – either a place kick or a drop kick from any point on the field of play on a line through the place where the *try* was scored. The kick must be

- taken without any time-wasting
- taken without any attempt to 'dummy' the opposition
- taken with everybody behind the ball at the time of the kick except when a placer is used

The opposition must stand behind their goal-line until the kicker begins his run or gestures that he is about to kick. Then they may jump or charge in an attempt to prevent the goal being scored but they must not shout. The referee will disallow the kick for any law-breaking by the kicker's team, and play will restart with a drop kick by the opposition at the centre of the half-way line. For an offence by the defending side the kick if successful will stand, or if it is unsuccessful the referee will allow the kick to be taken again without the defending side being allowed to charge.

Gareth Davies kicking a conversion for Cardiff.

OFFSIDE

During the normal course of play in a game of Rugby a player is in an offside position if the ball has been kicked or touched or is being carried by one of his team mates behind him. (For offside at the scrummage, line-out, ruck or maul refer to the sections dealing with these aspects of the game).

If you are in an offside position the referee will not stop the game unless you
- play the ball
- obstruct a member of the other side
- move towards or stay within 10 metres of a member of the other side who is waiting to play the ball or the place where the ball lands

Unless the other side gains some sort of advantage, if you do any of the things mentioned above, the referee will give a penalty kick to the other side at the place where you were offside.

There are times, however, when a player is not penalised for offside.
- *Accidentally offside* – where it is not possible to get out of the way of the ball or a player carrying it. The referee will only stop the game if the offside player's team gain an advantage from the situation. If they do, a scrummage will be given to the other side at the place where the offside occurred.
- When a player receives an unintentional forward pass.
- When because of the speed of the game a player cannot help being within 10 metres of an opponent waiting to play the ball, or the place where the ball lands, as long as he tries to move away as quickly as possible and without interfering with the other player.

During general play you are most likely to become offside when the ball is kicked ahead by one of your team mates.

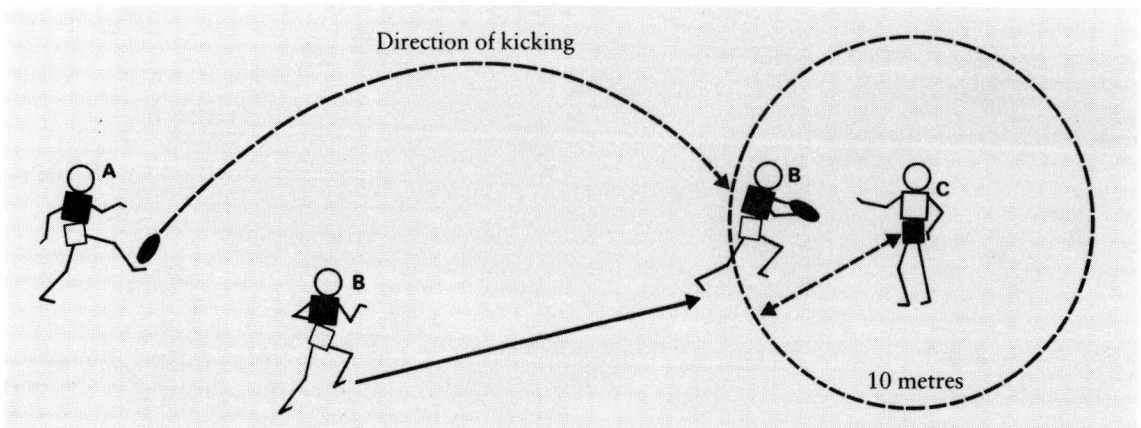

Direction of kicking

10 metres

At the time A kicks the ball forward, player B is in an offside position because the ball was last played by one of his team behind him. However, the referee will not stop the game unless B

(a) plays the ball as shown in the drawing
(b) obstructs an opponent
(c) moves towards or stays within 10 metres of an opponent C waiting to play the ball or the place where the ball lands.

What B should do is to get 10 metres away from the player waiting to play the ball as fast as he can.

When you are offside you cannot take part in the game but you can be put onside by your own team mates.

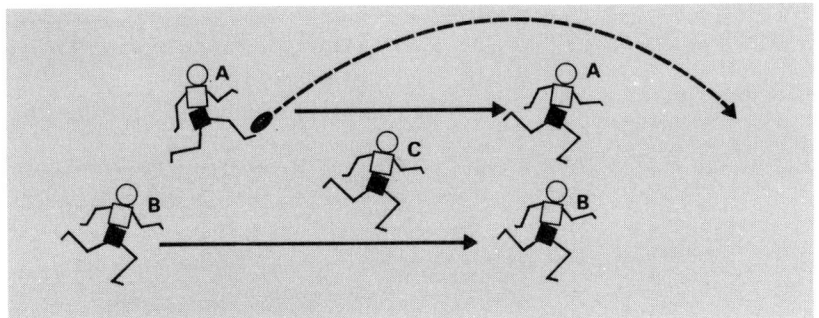

At the time the ball was kicked by A, C was offside but C can be put onside and so take part in the game again if A runs in front of him as shown. C can also be put onside by any other of his team mates who were onside when the ball was kicked (player B) as long as they too run ahead of him as shown.

Player A has the ball and is running towards his opponents' goal-line. Player C then is offside because the ball is being played by one of his team mates behind him, but C can be put onside again as long as his team mate with the ball runs ahead of him as shown.

In this situation A and B are onside and C is offside but C can put himself onside by running behind any of his onside team mates as shown. Once he is behind any of them he can take part in the game again.

You can also be put onside by the opposition (except if you are offside because you are within the 10-metre zone around a member of the other side waiting to play the ball or the place where the ball lands). In the situation shown, C is offside but he can be put onside by his opponent D, as long as D does one of these three things:

(a) carries the ball 5 metres as shown
(b) kicks or passes the ball
(c) deliberately touches it but does not hold it

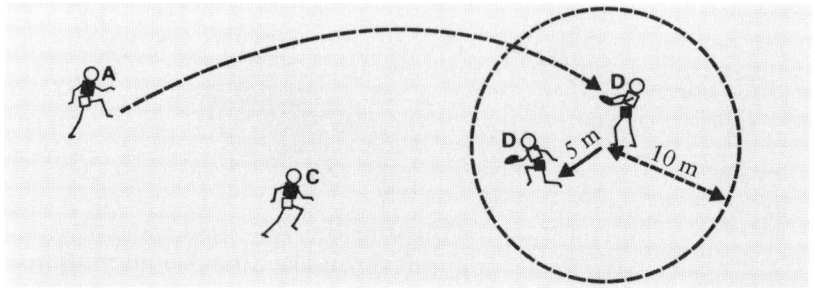

Thought and care must be taken not to get caught offside following scrums and line outs – as the ball is released the players must check their positions.

Remember, if you are offside leave the ball and the player alone!

FOUL PLAY

In Rugby referees take a very severe attitude towards players guilty of foul play. The result is a penalty kick or in some cases a penalty try to the opposition, and added to this the guilty player may be cautioned or sent off. Below are listed the different kinds of foul play.

Misconduct/dangerous play

This includes such things as hitting or kicking an opponent, late tackling, causing the scrummage to collapse, etc. The player may be sent off, or cautioned that he *will be* sent off if he repeats the offence. The referee will then award a penalty try to the opposition or a penalty kick at the place where the incident happened. The exceptions to this are:

- When someone has charged or obstructed a player who has just kicked the ball. Once this has happened the team given the penalty kick can take the kick at the place where the incident happened or take the kick where the ball lands. (See the diagram.)

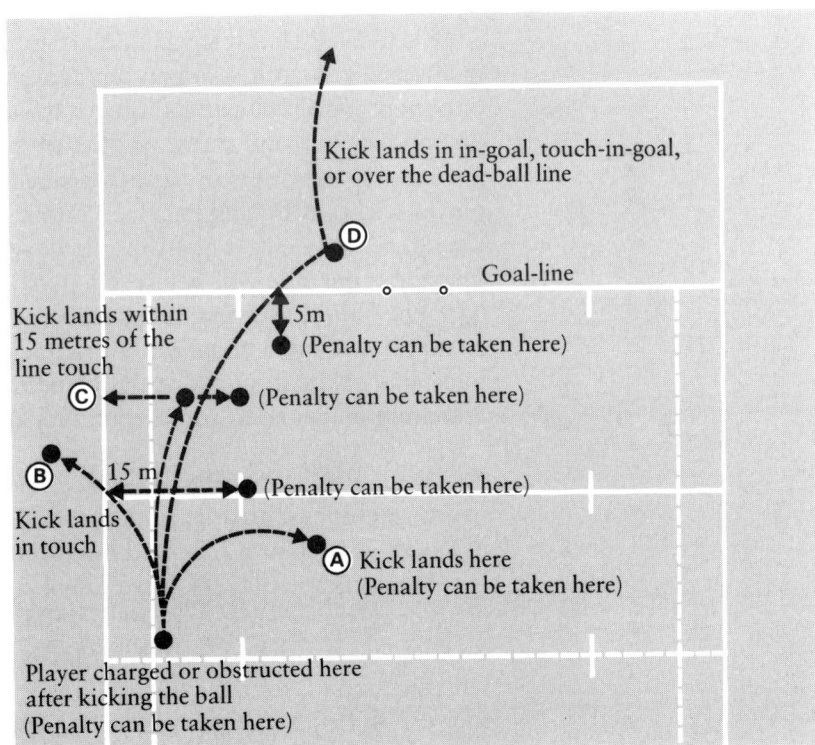

Kick lands in in-goal, touch-in-goal, or over the dead-ball line

Goal-line

Kick lands within 15 metres of the line touch

5m
(Penalty can be taken here)

(Penalty can be taken here)

15 m

(Penalty can be taken here)

Kick lands in touch

Ⓐ Kick lands here
(Penalty can be taken here)

Player charged or obstructed here after kicking the ball
(Penalty can be taken here)

The four situations, as shown, can be described as follows.

If the ball lands in the field of play (A) the mark is where the ball lands.

If the kick lands in touch (B) the mark is 15 metres in from touch.

If the kick lands within 15 metres of the touch line (C) the mark is 15 metres in from touch.

If the kick lands in in-goal, touch-in-goal or over the dead ball line (D) the mark is opposite the place where the ball crossed the goal-line and 5 metres from it. The kick is also taken 15 metres in from touch if the ball crosses the goal-line within 15 metres of the touch line. This means that if the ball crosses the goal-line near the posts the mark is 5 metres from the goal-line opposite the place where the ball crossed, but if it crosses near the corner flag the mark is 5 metres from the goal-line and 15 metres in from touch. When charging or obstructing a kicker happens in touch, the mark is given 15 metres in from the touch line opposite the place where the incident happened.

- When *misconduct* takes place while the ball is out of play the penalty kick is taken where the ball would next have been brought into play. If this is on or beyond the touch line the mark is brought 15 metres in from touch.

Obstruction

This means what it says. You are not allowed to obstruct members of the other side in any way, such as by pushing an opponent who is chasing a loose ball so that you can get to it first, or standing in front of one of your own players while offside and so stopping members of the other side from getting to the ball. If a player without the ball has been unfairly charged or obstructed the referee may either caution the player or send him off. In any case the other side will be given a penalty kick where the incident happened and in some cases a penalty try may be awarded, for example when in a chase with an attacking player to ground a loose ball in the in-goal area a defender deliberately obstructs the attacking player so as to prevent a try being scored.

Unfair play and other infringements

This includes cheating, time-wasting, deliberately throwing the ball off the pitch and repeated law-breaking. In cases of repeated law-breaking the players may be sent off or cautioned. However in all cases the referee will give a penalty kick at the place where the incident happened. A penalty try may also be given. Players who are sent off do not take any further part in the match and they are subject to very severe disciplinary action, such as being banned from playing for a long period of time.

THE LINE-OUT

If the ball touches the touch line or anything beyond it, the ball is then out of play. When the ball is out of play at the touch line we say it is *in touch*. The ball is also in touch when a player carrying it touches the touch line or the ground beyond it.

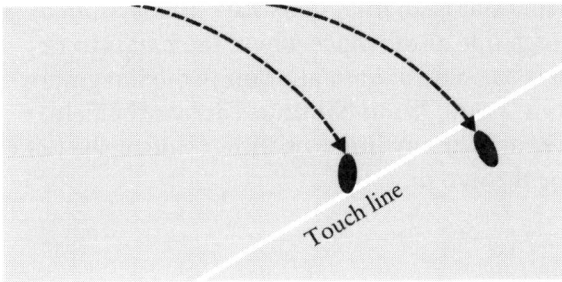

The ball is in touch if it touches the line or anything beyond it.

The ball is in touch when a player carrying it touches the touch line or the ground beyond it.

On the other hand, if the ball is not in touch a player who is in touch can kick or knock the ball with his hand as long as he does not hold it. Similarly if the ball crosses the touch line but does not touch the ground beyond it, a player on the pitch can catch it or knock it back into play (B).

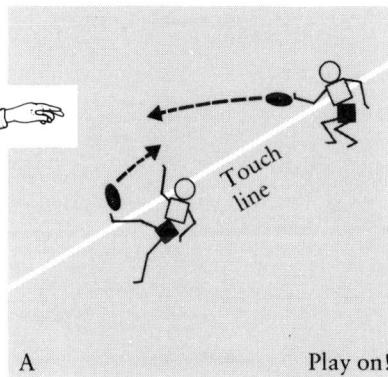

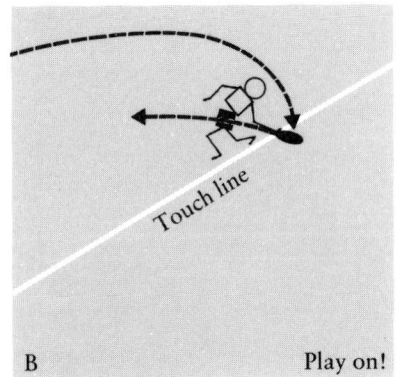

A   Play on!   B   Play on!

(A) In each case the player is in touch but the ball can still be played as long as it is not held.

The touch judge will indicate when the ball or a player carrying it has gone into touch and he does so by lifting one arm directly into the air with flag aloft while his other arm points to the team who have been given the throw-in.

The throw-in will take place at point X and the team playing from right to left will throw in.

When the ball has entered touch the game is restarted with a line-out. Where this takes place is decided by the way in which the ball went into touch, which in general is the place where the ball touched or crossed the touch line. The throw-in is given to the team who were not responsible for the ball going out of play; if there is any doubt, the attacking side are given the throw-in.

The line used in a line-out is an imaginary line (*line-of-touch*) at right angles to the touch line at the place where the ball is to be thrown in. If the ball is to be thrown in at point A the imaginary line we will use starts at point A and continues across the field. The same is true for B and for any point on either side of the field where the ball is to be thrown in.

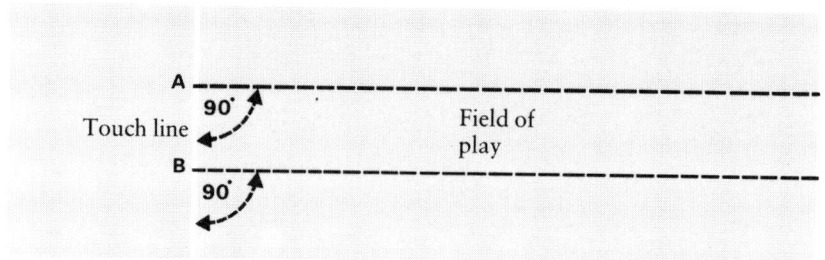

Where do the players stand?

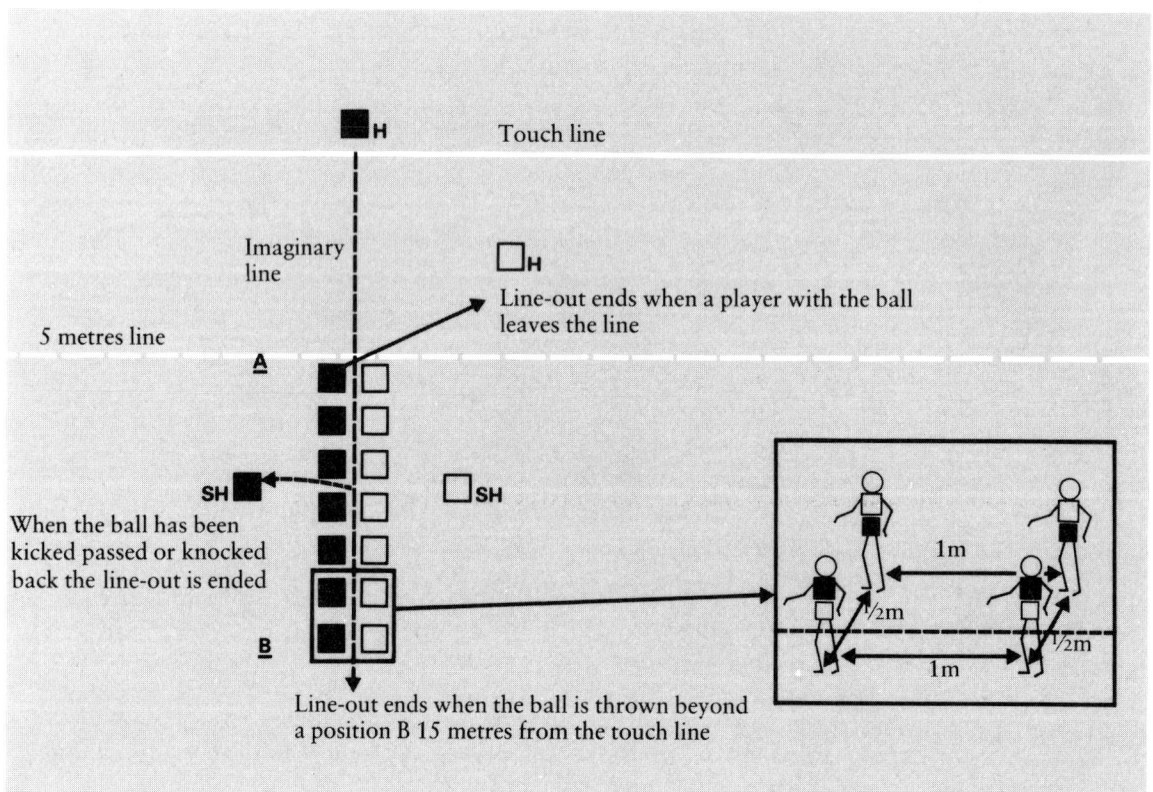

Touch line

Imaginary line

Line-out ends when a player with the ball leaves the line

5 metres line

When the ball has been kicked passed or knocked back the line-out is ended

Line-out ends when the ball is thrown beyond a position B 15 metres from the touch line

1m

½m

1m

½m

34

- At least two players from each pack of forwards line up in single lines parallel to the imaginary line with a clear space of ½ metre being left between the lines.
- If you are in the line-out your nearest team mate will be at least 1 metre away.
- The line-out stretches from point A to point B, A being 5 metres from the touch line, while point B is 15 metres from that touch line. The furthest player in the line-out of the team throwing the ball in can therefore be a maximum of 15 metres from the touch line. If any player is further than 15 metres from the touch line when the line-out starts, he is not in the line-out and is offside.
- The team throwing the ball in decide the maximum number of players from either team in the line-out. If this is less than normal, i.e. less than 7 men, the other side are allowed a short time to adjust to the correct number. As well as this, it is important to remember that a distance of at least 1 metre is required between players in the same team.

A free kick 15 metres from the touch line along the imaginary line-of-touch is awarded to the other side should any of the laws be broken.

Apart from the players in the lines the other players who are allowed to stand near the line-out are the scrum halves from either side (SH on the diagram) and the man throwing the ball in and his opposite number: these are generally the hookers from either side (H on the diagram).

Throwing the ball in

- The player throwing the ball in stands in touch at the place marked by the touch judge. When throwing the ball in, the thrower must not put any part of any foot in the field of play.
- The ball must be thrown in without any dummying action and also without wasting time.
- The ball must be thrown so that it travels at least 5 metres along the imaginary line before touching a player or the ground.
- The throw-in must be straight along the imaginary line.
- Once the line-out has begun, the player throwing the ball in, and his opposite number, must stay within 5 metres of the touch line, go back to the offside line, join in the line-out after the ball has been thrown in 5 metres or move into a position to receive the ball after it is passed or knocked back from the line-out.

If the throw-in is not correct, the other team are given the chance to have the throw-in at another line-out, or the put-in at a scrummage 15 metres in from touch along the line-of-touch.

If the first team make a mistake at a throw-in and the other side choose to have another line-out but they too make a mistake, a scrummage is awarded, with the put-in being given to the first team who made a mistake. The scrummage will take place 15 metres in from touch.

Quick throw-in

This is allowed provided that
- the same ball that went into touch is used
- the ball has been handled by the players only
- the throw-in is taken correctly

Note that at a quick throw-in the laws regarding the furthest player and the maximum 15 metres distance do not apply.

Once the line-out is formed

Players in the line-out must not leave their positions on one side of the imaginary line or the line-out itself until the line-out is finished except:
- when *peeling off* (see below)

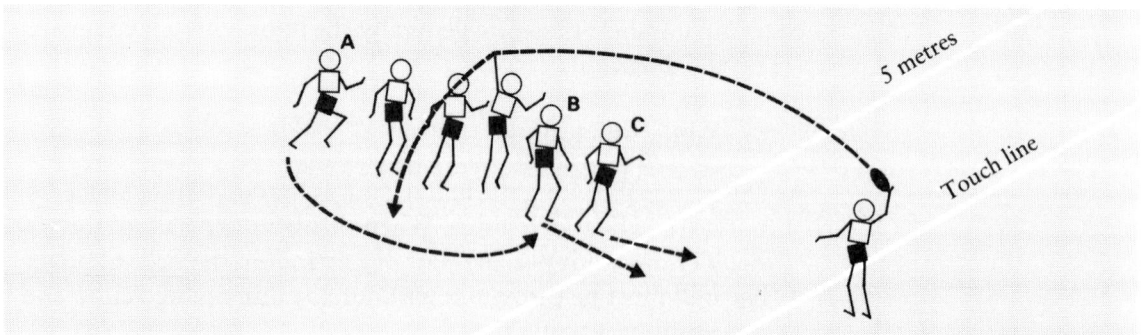

- at a quick throw-in (see above) where you can arrive and leave without being penalised
- when the team throwing the ball in lines up with less than the normal number; to adjust to the correct number, opposing players can leave as long as they quickly go behind their offside line

If you leave the line-out after it has formed the referee will give a free kick to the other side 15 metres in from touch along the imaginary line-of-touch.

Peeling off

This happens when a player moves from his place in the line-out so he can catch the ball when it has been passed or knocked back to him by a member of his team. The player must not begin to peel off until the ball has left the hands of the player throwing it in and when he does so he must move parallel and close to the line-out (see A). He must also keep moving until a ruck or maul is formed and he joins in it or the line-out ends. Players can move nearer than 5 metres to the thrower if the ball is thrown beyond them. However, unless they are taking part in a peeling-off movement, they must not move towards their own goal-line until the line-out ends. In the diagram, A has peeled off to take the tap down while B and C have moved towards the touch line to create a gap for A to run into.

For peeling-off offences the other side are given a free kick 15 metres in from touch along the line-of-touch.

What a player must not do at the line-out

Before the ball has been thrown in you must not
- make contact with any player from either side
- stand within 5 metres of the touch line
- stop the ball being thrown 5 metres
- be offside
- use any other player as an aid to jumping for the ball.

After the ball has been thrown in and has touched the ground or a player, you must not
- be offside
- charge an opponent except if you are tackling him or trying to play the ball
- push or pull or stand in the way of a member of the other side not holding the ball

Until the ball has been touched or has hit the ground players must remain 1 metre from the next player in their team and ½ metre from the opposition line except when peeling off or jumping for the ball.

Offside at the line-out

At a line-out there are two types of offside: for the players taking part in the line-out and for those players not taking part in the line-out.

Those players who are taking part in the line-out are shown inside the rectangle in the drawing, and these include both sets of forwards, the scrum halves, the man throwing the ball in and his opposite number. For these players the offside line is the imaginary line (line-of-touch) shown. A player is offside if

- Before the ball touches the ground or a player he moves over the imaginary line, unless he is jumping for the ball. As soon as the ball has been played the offside line runs through the ball itself, so you are offside if
- Either of your feet moves in front of the ball, unless you are carrying the ball or you are attempting a tackle, which must start from your side of the ball.
- When peeling off you do not keep close and parallel to the line.
- Before the line-out ends you move beyond a position 15 metres from the touch line. Players of the team throwing the ball in can move beyond this position for a long throw-in to them, provided they do not move until the ball is thrown. The opposition may then follow them.
- Players who move beyond a position 15 metres from the touch line in the expectation of a long throw in must be penalised if, for any reason, the ball is not thrown beyond 15 metres.

If you are guilty of any of the above the referee will give a penalty kick to the other side 15 metres from the touch line along the imaginary line-of-touch.

If he is not taking part in the line-out, a player is offside if, before the line-out has ended, he steps or stands with either foot in front of the imaginary offside lines marked in the drawing.

If you are guilty of stepping over the offside line the referee will give a penalty kick to the other side on your offside line at the place where you were offside but not less than 15 metres from the touch line.

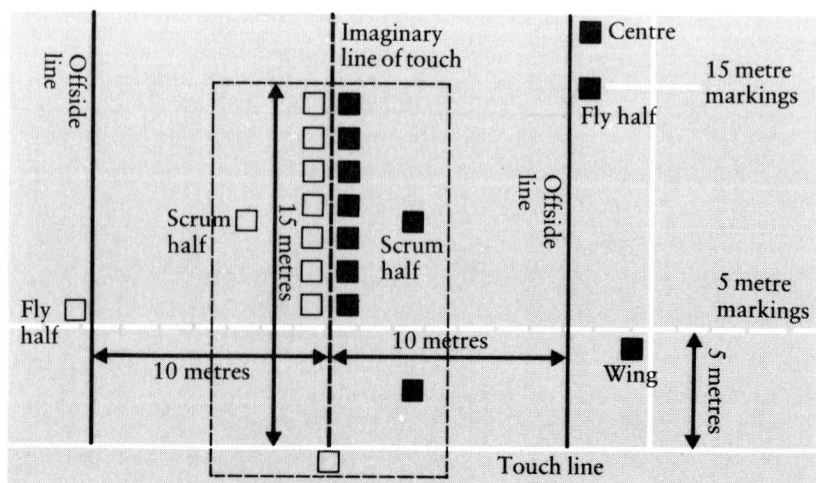

THE SCRUMMAGE

Where does a scrummage take place?

A scrummage takes place on the field of play as close as possible to the place where the law was broken. When the scrummage is near a goal-line, the front row of the defending team must be in the field of play before the ball is put in.

If the ball is on or over the goal-line in a scrummage, the scrummage is ended. When it is near the touch line the whole scrummage must be at least 5 metres from the touch line before the ball is put in.

Who takes part?

The forwards from either side take part. Normally eight players from either side are involved (the minimum number is 5).

How is it formed?

When the two teams come together and the middle line (which is an imaginary line directly beneath the shoulders of the two front rows) is parallel to the goal-lines.

Each team must abide by the following laws.
- The teams must allow the scrummage to be formed. If your team delays the formation of a scrummage the opposition are awarded a penalty kick.
- The scrummage must be still until the ball is put in. If your team moves before the ball is put in, i.e. pushes too early, the opposition are given a free kick.
- Each team must have a front row of three players at all times. If a team do not have a front row of three players, the other side are given a penalty kick.
- The two teams must not go down into the scrummage position until the ball is ready to be put in.

The players in the scrummage must not
- return the ball into the scrummage
- pick up the ball with their hands or legs or handle the ball while in the scrummage
- deliberately fall or kneel in the scrummage
- cause the scrummage to collapse

If any player is guilty of any one of the above the other side are given a penalty kick.

The front row players in the scrummage

The front row players must
- allow the ball to be put in and to touch the ground in the required place
- have both feet on the ground while the scrummage is forming and taking place so that they can push forwards

If any of the front row players break these laws the other side are given a free kick.

The front row players must not
- form down some distance away and rush against each other
- move their feet until the ball has touched the ground
- kick the ball out from where it came in
- lift both feet off the ground at any time
- have their head next to the head of a player in their own team

Breaking these laws will mean a penalty kick being awarded to your opponents — except in the case of moving the feet, where a free kick will be the result.

The other players in the scrummage

Other players in the scrummage must not
- Play the ball while it is in the 'tunnel' formed by the front rows. If the ball while in the tunnel is played by anyone other than the front row players the referee will give a free kick to the opposition.
- In the case of flank/wing forwards, they must not swing outwards with their hips while bound onto the scrummage in an attempt to obstruct the opposition scrum half. However, there is nothing to prevent you binding at an angle to the scrummage and so increasing the distance the opposing scrum half will have to run to get to the ball. If you swing out the referee will give a penalty kick to the other side.

Note, in all cases of penalty kicks and free kicks as a result of law-breaking at the scrummage the kick is taken at the place where the scrummage would originally have been formed.

Binding

Holding on to your team mates in the scrummage with one or two arms is called *binding*. In order to keep scrummages safe and steady, each player, depending on his position, is required to 'bind' on to a team mate, or on to a team mate and a member of the opposite team.

The binding of the props and the hooker is shown here. The hooker (no. 2) can bind over or under the arms of his props, grasping their shirts tightly around their bodies below armpit level. Binding over the arms of the props is often preferred, as it allows the hooker to release his binding in the case of a scrummage collapse and enables him to get nearer the ball when it is put in. The props (nos. 1 and 3) bind with the hooker in a similar manner.

The binding of the props with the opposition is as follows. The loose head prop (no. 1) can do one of two things:

- he can bind his opposing 'tight head' prop with his left arm inside the right arm of his opponent, or
- he can place his left hand or his forearm on his left thigh as shown in the drawing.

Note, he can also alter his binding at any time during the scrummage.

The tight head props (no. 3) must bind with with their right arms outside the left upper arms of their opposing loose head prop. It is worth remembering the simple phrases 'inside (tight head) bind outside' and 'outside (loose head) bind inside'. All other players must 'bind' with at least one arm and hand around the body of another player in the same team. This means that no player other than a prop may hold an opponent with his outer arm.

The second row players (nos. 4 and 5) bind to each other and also to their front row. The no. 8 binds on to his second row and the flank forwards (nos. 6 and 7) bind with their inside arms on to their second row team mates.

The put-in

The team who were not responsible for the stoppage of play put the ball in. If there is any doubt, the team who were moving forward at the time, or, if play was a standstill, the attacking side have the put-in.

The ball is put in without any delay as soon as the two front rows have come together when ordered to by the referee. If a team delay putting the ball into a scrummage the referee will give a penalty kick to the other side.

The scrum half must do the following to ensure that he will put the ball in correctly
- stand 1 metre from the scrummage
- stand midway between the two front rows
- hold the ball in two hands
- hold the ball at a level between his knee and ankle

If he fails to do any of these things the other side are given a free kick.

The ball is put in as follows:
- with a single forward movement on the side first chosen (although it is very rare to opt to put the ball in from your own 'tight head' side)
- straight along the middle (imaginary) line
- so that it touches the ground immediately beyond the nearest prop's shoulders

Failure to do any of these things means the other side will be awarded a free kick.

The ball 'comes out' when a player of either front row uses his foot to gain possession. Once the ball is hooked (heeled backwards) players are only allowed to use their feet or lower legs to move the ball. When the ball is in the scrummage the scrum half is not allowed to kick it; if he does, the other team will be awarded a penalty kick. If the ball comes out of either end of the tunnel, the same team are allowed to put the ball in again.

Offside at the scrummage

The offside line at the scrummage is an imaginary line through the back foot of your back player in the scrummage and is parallel to the goal-lines as shown in the drawing opposite. Any player apart from the scrum halves and the players in the scrummage must stay behind this line until the ball comes out. These players are offside if while the scrummage is forming or taking place they:

Offside line

- join the scrummage from their opponents' side
- fail to go behind the offside line or their goal-line, whichever is nearer
- place either foot in front of the offside line while the ball is in the scrummage

A player is allowed to leave the scrummage as long as

- he is behind the ball and
- he immediately goes behind the offside line.

A player can also rejoin the scrummage. However, he must do so behind the ball. He is not allowed to play the ball as it emerges between the feet of his front row if he is in front of the offside line. With the ball in position A in the drawing, no. 7 can leave the scrummage as long as he goes immediately behind the offside line. However, if before he gets behind the offside line the ball comes out at, say, point B he is not allowed to move forward and play the ball.

Remember, remain in the scrummage unless you are the rearmost player i.e. no. 8 or a flank forward in a *wheeling scrummage*. Leaving the scrummage to take part in a special tactic is very difficult to time and requires coaching and practice. Leave this to the top-class players.

However, when the scrummage is being wheeled (when, after the ball has been put in, the whole scrummage begins to turn clockwise) the offside line (the back foot of the hindmost player in either side) also changes. In the diagram the offside line began as being the back feet of the respective no. 8 forwards. However, because of the clockwise motion the offside line now runs through the back feet of the respective no. 7 players. In a straight scrummage the back foot of the no. 8 players would be the offside lines in each case.

Touch line

Wheeling

Offside line

Offside line

The player who puts the ball in to the scrummage (the scrum half) can also be offside if, while the ball is in the scrummage, he stays, or places either foot, in front of the ball.

For offside at the scrummage a penalty kick is given to the opposition at the place where the offside happened.

RUCKS AND MAULS

A ruck

This happens when
- the ball is on the ground
- one or more players from each team are in contact with each other, while standing up, with the ball between them
- the ball is in the field of play (if the ball is in in-goal the ruck is ended).

A player joining a ruck must bind with at least one arm round the body of a team mate taking part in the ruck. At a ruck a player must not
- handle the ball or pick it up
- jump on top of other players or deliberately collapse the ruck
- return the ball into the ruck
- deliberately fall down or kneel down
- while on the ground, play the ball

If a player breaks any of the above laws the referee will give a penalty kick to the other team at the spot where the law is broken.

Remember, at a ruck, stay on your feet, use your eyes, and drive forward.

A maul

This happens when
- the ball is in the field of play (if the ball is in in-goal the maul is ended)
- one or more players from each team, while standing up, are in contact with a player who is carrying the ball

At a maul you must not jump on other players and you must be bound on to or caught up in the maul.

If you just hang around at a maul or jump on the players in it the referee will give a penalty kick at the spot where the law was broken.

Remember, at a maul do not hang around: bind on, look for the ball and drive forward.

A maul ends when the ball is on the ground or when a player carrying the ball leaves it. If the ball takes a while to emerge from a maul or ruck, the referee will give the put-in at a scrummage to the team who were not responsible for the stoppage, or, if there is a doubt, the team who were moving forward at the time. If everybody was at a standstill the attacking side are given the put-in.

Offside

At a ruck or maul the offside line is an imaginary line through the back foot of the hindmost player in the ruck or the maul. This line is parallel to the goal-lines.

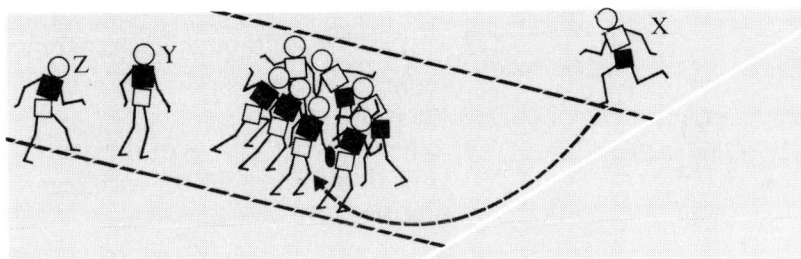

In the diagram a ruck has developed around the ball. The offside line for each team is indicated. A player is offside when a ruck or maul is taking place
- if he joins from his opponents' side, as shown by player X
- if he joins it in front of the ball
- if he does not join in but fails to quickly get behind his offside line, as shown by player Y
- if he leaves the ruck or maul and does not quickly rejoin it or get behind his offside line
- if he steps with either foot beyond his offside line but does not join in, as shown by player Z

If a player is offside on any of the above counts the referee will give a penalty kick to the other side at the place where the law was broken.

When a ruck or maul takes place at a line-out the players taking part in the line-out are not forced to take part in the ruck or maul but must continue to take part in the line-out until the line-out is ended.

When a line-out is happening which results in a ruck or maul being formed, a player is offside if he joins the ruck or maul from his opponents' side or if he joins it in front of the ball. He is also offside if he is still taking part in the line-out but not in the ruck or maul if he does not go back to his offside line (behind the back foot of his team mates taking part in the ruck or maul).

If these laws are broken the other side get a penalty kick 15 metres from the touch line along the imaginary line-of-touch.

A player is also offside if he is not taking part in the ruck or maul if he stays or moves forward beyond his offside line. The referee will give a penalty kick to the other side on their opponents' offside line at a spot which is opposite the place where the law was broken, but not less than 15 metres in from touch.

THE REFEREE AND THE TOUCH JUDGES

Every match should have a referee and two touch judges. The referee

- keeps time – although he may sometimes consult his touch judges
- keeps score
- applies fairly the laws of the game – although he may sometimes consult his touch judges with regard to misconduct and dangerous play

When a situation occurs which is beyond the control of the referee and which is not covered in the laws of the game, such as when a dog runs on to the pitch and bursts the ball the game will be stopped. The game will be restarted with a scrummage, the put-in being given to the team who were moving forward at the time or, when neither team are moving forward, to the attacking side.

Once the referee has made a decision it cannot be altered except when

- the decision was made before the referee saw a touch judge with his flag raised
- the decision was made before the referee received a report from a touch judge regarding misconduct or dangerous play

The touch judges signalling a successful conversion attempt – England have just scored against Wales.

46

With regard to the game itself the referee is in complete control, being responsible for both the conduct and the safety of the players. This means that the referee has the power to end the match before all the playing time has been used up if he considers that to continue playing would be dangerous (e.g. during a violent electric storm) or that for some reason the full time cannot be played (e.g. when the light becomes so poor that seeing the ball is difficult).

No matter what the decision, all players must accept it. In order to stop the game and in order to start the game at the beginning of each half the referee will blow his whistle. The final time the whistle is blown during the game is when all the playing time has been used up and in Rugby we call this *no-side*. The ball has to be 'dead' before the whistle can be blown to signal half-time or no-side. If the ball is dead the referee will blow his whistle. If the ball is still in play he will blow his whistle when the ball next becomes dead except:

- if the next time the ball becomes dead it is after a try has been scored (then he will allow the conversion to be taken and then he will blow his whistle)
- if it next becomes dead when a fair catch, free kick or penalty has been given (then he will let play continue till the next time the ball becomes dead, when he will blow his whistle)

Because the referee is continuously involved in the game it is very likely that at some stage he will make contact with the ball. When this happens play is allowed to continue unless the referee decides that either team has gained an advantage. If a team gain an advantage, the referee will award a scrummage, the put-in being given to the team who last played the ball.

There should be two touch judges for every match and they should both carry flags. Their main job is to signal when the ball goes into touch. When the ball is put back into play they lower their flags except when

- the wrong team puts the ball in
- the player putting the ball in steps onto the field of play

Although the touch judges signal when the ball goes into touch, it is up to the referee to decide the correct place for the throw-in. In fact, the touch judges are completely under the control of the referee. They have to remain in touch for the whole game except when judging a kick at goal, when they are required to stand behind the goal-posts. If the goal is good they have to signal. Other than that, however, they have no other involvement in the game except in international matches, where they are allowed to report incidents of dangerous play or misconduct to the referee.

What the referee will expect from you

You should always
- respect the authority of the referee – accepting his decisions
- remain silent after a decision has been made – not questioning it
- stop playing as soon as the referee blows his whistle
- allow the referee to inspect your equipment and the way you are dressed.

   (This is to make sure that you are not wearing anything that might be dangerous to yourself or to other players, such as rings, watches, boots with sharp-edged studs etc. There are times when the referee may ask you to replace a badly torn jersey or shorts in case they fall apart while you are playing. However, there is no need to worry about being asked to leave the field if your jersey is suddenly ripped off your back. The referee will allow time when the ball is dead for you to change into a fresh jersey or shorts. What you need to remember is that you are not allowed any time to re-tie or replace your boot laces, so make sure the laces are sound and tied tightly)
- ask the permission of the referee to leave the field of play or re-enter the field of play, as happens during cases of injury

If a player starts playing again without the permission of the referee, and his side gains an advantage through his actions, the referee will decide if the player's action was deliberate or not. In the case of it not being deliberate, he will give a scrummage with the other side having the put-in at the place where he started playing again without permission.

If on the other hand the referee decides that the player's action was deliberate then he will award a penalty kick to the other side. The referee will give the same decision in all cases of misconduct (misbehaviour) by the players.

A referee awarding a try.

Equipment

The drawing shows what you can and cannot wear when playing rugby.

Ear-rings or studs are not allowed

A headband or skull-cap to protect the ears can be worn

Spectacles should not be worn

A gum-shield is advisable as it protects your teeth and head

Team jersey with reinforced collar

Reinforced cotton shorts

All items of jewellery rings, watches etc. must be removed

The ball

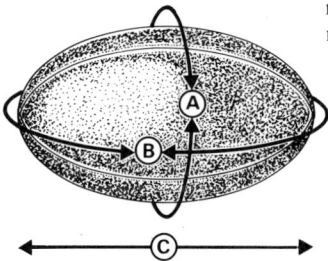

Oval-shaped, weight 400–440 gms, pressure 9½–10lb/sq inch A 580–620 mm
B 760–790 mm
C 280–300 mm

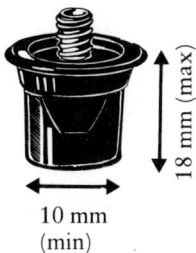

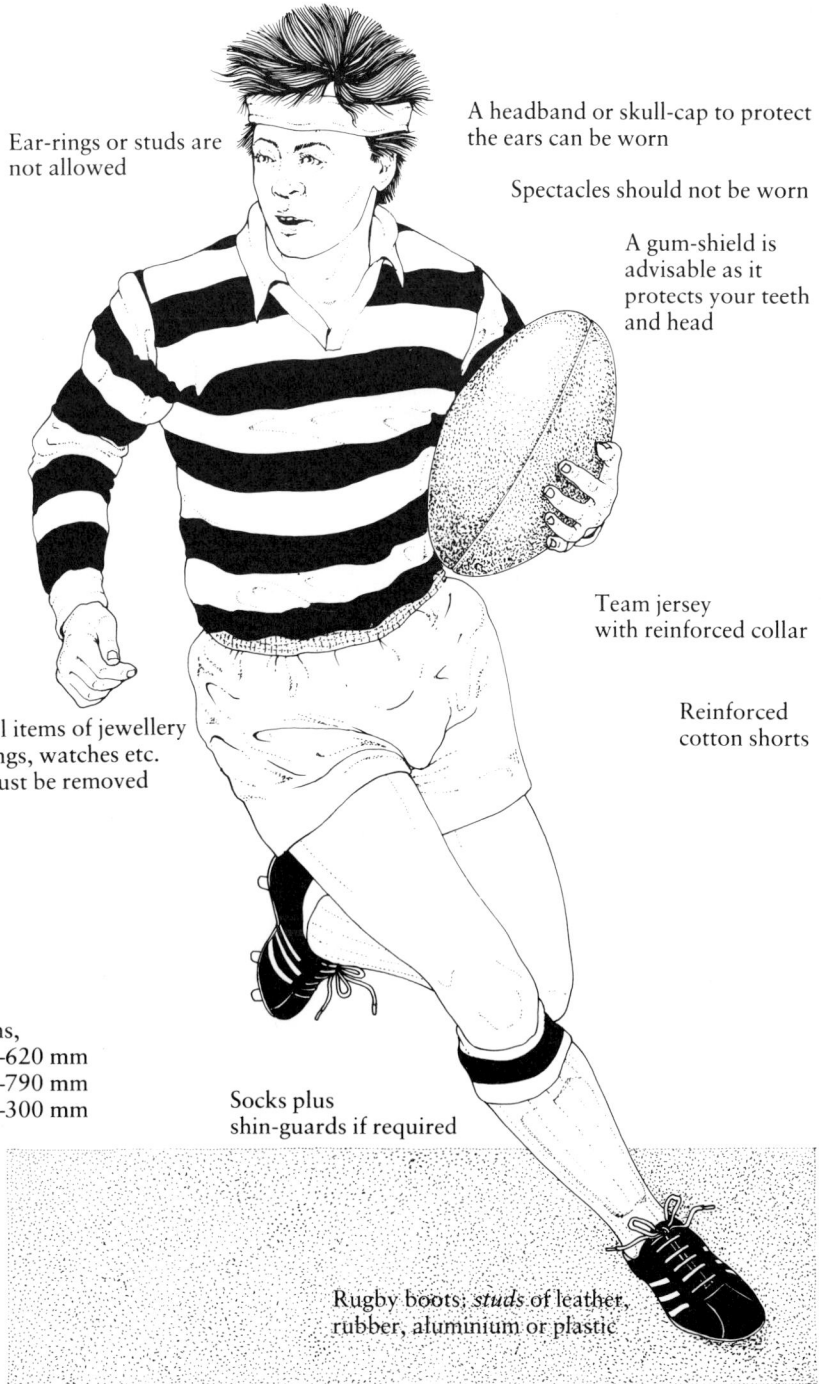

Socks plus shin-guards if required

18 mm (max)

10 mm (min)

Rugby boots; *studs* of leather, rubber, aluminium or plastic

WHAT POSITION SHALL I PLAY?

When you first start to play Rugby you will probably want to try out most of the playing positions so that you can then decide which position best suits your physique, strength, speed, skills and temperament. To help you decide you should also watch more experienced players as well as asking the advice of your coach.

You will find by watching other Rugby matches that each player has a particular job to do and in order to do that job well he requires certain qualities. The special qualities required for each of the positions are described below. Look carefully at these as it may help you decide which playing position will suit you best.

Who's turn to wash the kit?

The forwards

Their combined role has been described earlier, however each member of the pack has a special job during the game as well as having to perform all the basic skills.

Prop forward (numbers 1 and 3)

Jobs

- to act as a cornerstone of the scrummage
- to support your hooker
- to withstand the shove of the opposition
- to act as the front line of the shove for your own forwards

Qualities

Toughness, strength and the ability to move quickly around the field. A stocky, well-built player is required.

Hooker (number 2)

Jobs

- to strike the ball cleanly in the scrummage
- to throw the ball in at the line-out

Qualities

Quick reactions, strength, flexibility. A strong supple player is required.

Second row (numbers 4 and 5)

Jobs

- to act as the main shove of the scrummage
- to win the ball at the line-out

Qualities

Strength, jumping ability and the ability to move quickly around the field. A tall strong heavy player is required.

Wing forward (numbers 6 and 7)

Jobs

- to create and support attacks for and by your own team
- to eliminate the effectiveness of the opponents' fly half and scrum half
- to create attacks from opponents' mistakes
- to be an effective tackler in all situations
- to keep up with the play at all times

Qualities

Strength, speed, tackling ability. A fast strong hard-tackling player is required.

Number 8

Jobs
- Adding extra power to the scrummage.
- Winning the ball at the line-out.
- Supporting attacks.
- Covering in defence.

Qualities

Strength, speed, aggression, jumping ability. A tall strong fast-moving player is required.

The backs

Their combined role has been described earlier; however, each player is expected to perform specialist functions other than the basic skills.

Scrum-half (number 9)

Jobs

- to act as the link between the forwards and backs
- to use the ball intelligently
- to put the ball in at the scrummage

Qualities

Quick thinking, quick reactions, speed off the mark, passing ability. A player with quick reflexes and good passing ability in all situations is required.

Fly half (number 10)

Jobs
- to make tactical decisions at a moment's notice
- to use the ball intelligently

Qualities

Quick reactions, speed, kicking and passing ability, ability to make split-second decisions. A player who can read the game and who can kick and pass effectively is required.

Centre (numbers 12 and 13)

Jobs

- to create openings in the opposition's defensive line
- to prevent the opposition breaking through the defensive line

Qualities

Speed, tackling ability, quick reactions. A player who can run well with the ball and who can tackle at speed is required.

Wing (numbers 11 and 14)

Jobs
- to run with speed and determination towards the opponents' goal-line whenever the ball is received
- to act as a covering player in defence and to prevent the opposition breaking through the defensive line

Qualities

Speed, determination, ability to change pace and direction. A player who can run with the ball at full speed is required.

Full back (number 15)

Jobs
- to be well positioned to counteract all the opposition's attacking moves
- to act as an extra attacking player as the situation arises
- to catch and kick the ball cleanly in all defensive situations

Qualities

Ability to read the game, positional sense, a cool head in all situations, catching and kicking ability. A player who can read game situations and react accordingly is required.

TEST YOUR KNOWLEDGE

1 What do they call the player who wears –
   a) the no. 2 shirt,
   b) the no. 9 shirt,
   c) the no. 15 shirt?
2 How many points are you awarded if you score a try?
3 Which lines border the 'field of play'?
4 If you see a Law being broken why must you never wait for the whistle?
5 From where do we take the kick-off?
6 When a kick-off is taken after an unconverted *try* what type of kick is used?
7 What decision does the referee make when your team knock on, and the other side do not gain an advantage?
8 When are the two occasions when you can knock on and get away with it?
9 What is a tackle?
10 When is the only time you need not release the ball when you are held and brought to the ground?
11 What happens if an attacker kicks the ball over your goal-line and you ground it?
12 What happens if an attacker grounds a loose ball in your in-goal area?
13 What are the conditions required of you when calling for a mark?
14 A player kicks a ball *directly* into touch. From where would the ball be put in for the line out if:
   a) the player kicked the ball from within his 22-metre line?
   b) the player kicked the ball from outside his 22-metre line?
15 Which of these kicks are you allowed to charge –
   a) penalty kick,
   b) conversion,
   c) free kick?
16 What must you do if a penalty kick is awarded against your team?
17 At a free kick, when can you begin to charge the kicker?
18 During the normal course of the game, when are you in an off-side position?
19 If you are in front of a team mate and he kicks the ball and then chases it, when do you become onside again?
20 If a player is guilty of foul play what does the referee do?

21 If you deliberately stand in front of a player running to ground a loose ball in your in-goal area and you prevent a try being scored, what action will the referee take?
22 If the ball lands on the touch line is it out of play?
23 How far can the line-out stretch?
24 Who decides how many players will take part in the line-out?
25 When does a line-out start?
26 For the players not taking part in the line-out where is the offside line?
27 How is a scrummage formed?
28 Are you allowed to pick up the ball while it is in the scrummage?
29 What is 'binding'?
30 Where must the scrum half stand and how must he put the ball in at a scrummage?
31 Where is the offside line at the scrummage?
32 When does a ruck occur?
33 How many players are required to make up a maul?
34 When does a maul end?
35 Where is the offside line at a ruck or maul?
36 What must the touch judges do when a team is attempting a kick at goal?
37 How much time will the referee allow you to recover from an injury before he asks you to leave the field?
38 Why must you check your boot laces before each game?
39 What must you do as soon as you hear the whistle?
40 If you have to leave the field for any reason what must you do?

ANSWERS

1. a) the hooker b) the scrum half c) the full back.
2. Four points.
3. The touch lines and the goal-lines.
4. Because the referee will probably wait to see if the team who were not at fault can gain an advantage from the situation.
5. At the mid-point of the half-way line.
6. Drop kick.
7. He awards a scrummage to the opposition at the place where the knock-on occurred.
8. a) When charging down an opponent's kick.
   b) When you mess up your catch but can still catch the ball before it touches the ground or another player.
9. A tackle is when you hold the man carrying the ball by any part of his body or clothing so that while you are holding him he is brought to the ground or the ball hits the ground.
10. When, although tackled correctly at the same instant, you are knocked over your opponents' goal-line and a try is scored.
11. Your team are awarded a 22-metre drop-out.
12. The attackers' team are awarded a try.
13. a) You must be inside your own 22-metre line.
    b) The ball must be caught cleanly from a kick, knock-on or throw forward by the other side.
    c) You must be standing still with both feet on the ground.
    d) You must shout 'Mark' at the same time as you catch the ball.
14. a) At the point where the ball crossed the touch line.
    b) At the point opposite the place from where the ball was kicked.
15. b) and c)
16. Immediately go back 10 metres and stand still and silent until the kick has been taken.
17. As soon as he begins to run, or as soon as he has made a gesture that he is about to kick the ball.
18. If the ball has been kicked or touched or is being carried by a team mate who is behind you.
19. When the man who kicked the ball runs in front of you.
20. The referee awards a penalty kick, or in some cases a penalty try, to the opposition. Added to this the guilty player may be cautioned or sent off.
21. The referee will award a penalty try to the opposition and you may be cautioned or sent off.

22 Yes.

23 A maximum of 15 metres from the touch line.

24 The team throwing the ball in.

25 When the ball has left the hands of the player throwing it in.

26 A line parallel with the goal-lines, 10 metres from the imaginary line-of-touch.

27 When the two sets of forwards come together and the middle line is parallel to the goal-lines.

28 No.

29 Holding on to your team mates in the scrummage with one or two arms.

30 He must stand one metre from the scrummage midway between the two front rows. With the ball held in two hands at a level between his knee and ankle he must put it in with a single forward movement straight along the middle line so that it touches the ground immediately beyond the nearest prop's shoulders.

31 An imaginary line parallel to the goal-lines through the back foot of a player's team in the scrummage.

32 When the ball is in play, on the ground, and one or more players from each team are in contact with each other while standing up, with the ball between them.

33 One or more players from each team plus the man who is carrying the ball.

34 When the ball is on the ground or when a player carrying the ball leaves the maul.

35 An imaginary line parallel with the goal-lines through the back foot of the player's team in the ruck or the maul.

36 They must stand behind the goal posts so that they can signal to the referee whether or not the kick is successful.

37 Unless there are special circumstances, you are only allowed one minute to recover.

38 Because the referee will not allow any time during the game should you need to re-fasten them.

39 Stop playing and listen for the referee's decision.

40 Ask the permission of the referee.